THE CONTINUOUSLY IMPROVING SELF

A Personal Guide to TQM

Jeffrey E. Lickson, Ph.D.

CRISP PUBLICATIONS, INC.
Los Altos, California

THE CONTINUOUSLY IMPROVING SELF

A Personal Guide to TQM

Jeffrey E. Lickson, Ph.D.

CREDITS:
Editor: **Kay Kepler**
Designer: **Carol Harris**
Typesetting: **ExecuStaff**
Cover Design: **Carol Harris**
Artwork: **Ralph Mapson**

Copyright © 1992 Crisp Publications, Inc.
Printed in the United States of America by Bawden Printing Company.

English language Crisp books are distributed worldwide. Our major international distributors include:

CANADA: Reid Publishing, Ltd., Box 69559—109 Thomas St., Oakville, Ontario Canada L6J 7R4. TEL: (416) 842-4428; FAX: (416) 842-9327

AUSTRALIA: Career Builders, P.O. Box 1051, Springwood, Brisbane, Queensland, Australia 4127. TEL: 841-1061, FAX: 841-1580

NEW ZEALAND: Career Builders, P.O. Box 571, Manurewa, Auckland, New Zealand. TEL: 266-5276, FAX: 266-4152

JAPAN: Phoenix Associates Co., Mizuho Bldg. 2-12-2, Kami Osaki, Shinagawa-Ku, Tokyo 141, Japan. TEL: 3-443-7231, FAX: 3-443-7640

Selected Crisp titles are also available in other languages. Contact International Rights Manager Tim Polk at (415) 949-4888 for more information.

Library of Congress Catalog Card Number 91-77764
Lickson, Jeffrey E.
The Continuously Improving Self
ISBN 1-56052-151-1

This book is printed on recyclable paper with soy ink.

INTRODUCTION

Machines break. Some assets earn no interest or dividends. Some lose money. Much in our lives is outside of our control. So what do we control? The most important asset we possess is potentially within our control: namely ourselves.

Everything in the world is unique. Everything is slightly different from every other thing. Understand the reasons for these differences and you possess "profound knowledge" (Deming, 1989). With this knowledge, you can predict, manage and guide some of the processes that cause variation.

This book is designed to help you understand some of the reasons for these differences, including natural or random variation. We will explore the principles of W. Edwards Deming, a statistician who has written widely on the concept of quality. Then we will apply these quality principles personally, because individuals are the most important unit of change.

This books cuts deeper than most presentations about quality management. It addresses some of the personal issues in us that interfere with our ability to fully participate in organization change efforts. It is designed to help us better understand and influence the quality of our lives.

This book will increase the assets you bring to your job. Every organization wants employees that bring these Continuously Improving personal attributes:

- positive self-esteem

- creative energy for discovering how to improve processes at work and home

- increased feelings of power and influence

- increased ability to hear the "voice of the customer" and to serve others

- clearly communicated wants and flexible, cooperative strategies for achieving them

The continuously improving self is for people seeking quality at work or at home. A continuously improving self is capable of regeneration, enormous appreciation and contributing incalculable resources to your organizations, to their families and to quality relationships.

i

This path is simple, yet unending. You must choose how long, how intensively and how far you wish to journey for the continuously improving you. You must also understand that self-improvement is both a journey and an unreachable destination.

Self-discovery means examining your comfort zones, your habits, likes, dislikes, relationships, hopes and fears. When you finish this book, you should have a clearer idea of who you are, what you want and how you can improve.

Jeffrey E. Dickson

ACKNOWLEDGMENTS

I gratefully acknowledge the inspiration and help of my parents, my wise and loving wife, Nancy, my children, grandchildren, family, friends and clients.

Many ideas in this book come from teachers and writers such as: W. Edwards Deming's 14 obligations of management; William Conway's "Right Way to Manage"; William Dyer and Phil Daniel's ideas about professional development; Stephen Covey's "Seven Habits of Highly Effective People"; Leo Buscaglia's commitment to teaching people how to live, love and learn; Otto Rank, Felix Biestek, Jessie Taft and Anita Faatz's ideas about professional self, relationships and the nature of personal choice.

This book comes out of 28 years of working with people, learning from them and observing many good people blocked from quality because they were not empowered, by themselves or others.

Special thanks are due to participants in the October, 1991, Continuously Improving Self workshop pilot evaluation, where we tested and upgraded the ideas and exercises in this book: Rebecca Campbell, American General Life Insurance Co.; Tom Lewalski, Brown & Root, Inc.; Gregg Stocker, Ruska Instrument Corp.; Judy Dawson and Norma Martinez, City of Houston, Dept. of Public Utilities; George Huxel, Leadership Studies, International; David Harrison, Harrison Partners; and Pat Herron, Training Consortium.

We remain each other's customers and suppliers. Thank you for your generous help. Let's keep climbing up the path of continuous quality improvement—together.

CONTENTS

P A R T

1

The Concept

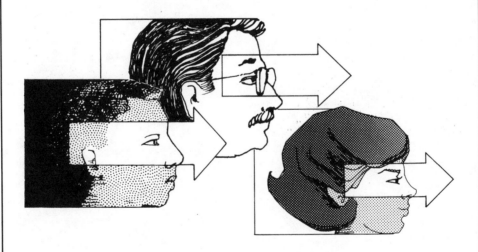

Who could resist hiring, promoting or passionately loving the quality person each of us has the potential to be? What is the path for becoming such a person? The path for a continuously improving self is different for each of us. We each bring our individual story of who we were, who we are now, and who we wish to be in the future.

TOM'S STORY

Tom, age 36, was a teacher, salesman and small business owner before joining Lightspeed Computers as a store manager. Tom currently supervises eight sales associates, four computer technicians, and two customer service clerks. Lightspeed Computers buys and sells inexpensive personal computers, printers and software for home and business use. It is a growing company that has expanded from one to forty-three stores. Lightspeed Computers is currently teaching its managers Total Quality Management.

Tom has always enjoyed people and dreaded numbers. He was an average student who got by on his energy and capacity to communicate and amuse others. Tom has been married to a graphics artist for ten years. They have two daughters and a happy home. His wife still laughs at his jokes.

Tom's store is located in a small shopping center in a declining middle class neighborhood. In his three years as manager, his store's sales volume initially increased, but has remained constant for the past seven months.

Tom is worried. In the past, he often experienced early success, only to be met with more difficult challenges later. He left teaching because he did not want to go back to school to take the required Continuing Education credits. He moved from selling computers to running a small PC support business so he could ''keep more of the money.'' He quickly discovered that his disdain for details was fatal. The business failed in eight months, in spite of growing sales. Tom could not manage cash flow or trust someone else to keep his books.

Tom's parents are both lifelong educators. Thrifty, they hold a self-professed disinterest in business. Tom never feels he is good enough to win his father's approval. When stressed at work, Tom feels inadequate and often wisecracks, to cope with his pain. Tom works hard and cares about his family and business associates, but he has been resisting the company's enthusiasm for TQM.

Finally, he concludes that the way things have been going, he has nothing to lose by trying TQM. This book will follow Tom's learning journey.

The exercises in this book are designed to help you discover your individual path for a continuously improving self. Think of your journey as an arduous, exciting adventure.

Eight Choices for a Continuously Improving You

I will:	I am ready	Not ready yet
1. Think about my past, present and future		
2. Create energy for changing my old thoughts and for trying new habits		
3. Invest time and energy building quality relationships		
4. Empower myself and others to ask questions and make mistakes		
5. Invest energy in self-understanding and self-mastery		
6. Study, gather information, keep an open mind and seek profound knowledge		
7. Help others learn about and from me		
8. Grant myself and others amnesty so we can enjoy our work and personal lives		

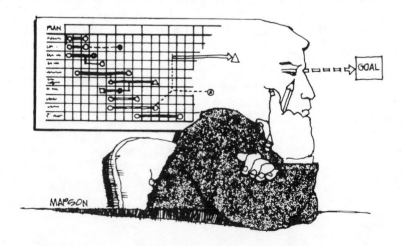

PERSONAL DEFINITIONS OF QUALITY

A continuously improving you implies ongoing awareness of the gap between where you are in your overall human performance, and where you wish to be.

Our desired improvements are part of our personal definition of quality. We are our own customer seeking these improvements. As with all other customers, we must make a distinction between the qualities we desire and our imperfect selves, the quality message and the messenger.

The very act of defining what we want activates internal and external barriers to achieving them. Bone and Griggs (1989) defined personal quality standards as the tests we use on ourselves and others to see if we do what we said we would do. Often it is difficult to sort out the following parts of our quest toward self-mastery:

- Individual potential
- Interference from others
- Environmental limits
- Beliefs about ourselves
- Profound knowledge
- Interpersonal dynamics

Scott and Jaffee (1991) suggested that managers with new mindsets, relationships and organizational structures can build an empowered work force. They recognized that the manager was a key element in creating this new workplace. They also recognized that both managers and employees must rethink old ways and learn new ones. Bone and Griggs (1989) viewed commitment, competence and communication as the three intangible basics of our personal and organizational quality goals.

Most of us have the individual potential to learn competence at work and in our personal lives. Making a commitment for a continuously improving self may require changes in our beliefs about ourselves, increased understanding of our perception of interference from others and our environmental limits. There is no profound knowledge without effective learning, communication from the external world through all of our previous learning, filters and beliefs to new thoughts and actions. We are the instrument through which organizational or personal quality messages must pass. The rest of this book will help us understand the message, the messenger and the ongoing struggle to keep ourselves motivated for continuous improvement.

P A R T

2

Deciding Where
to Begin

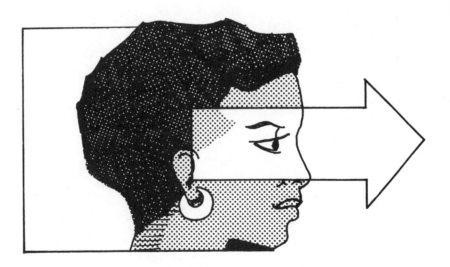

As a person seeking quality, it is important to assess the strengths and barriers that keep you from achieving the personal and work improvements you desire.

SELF-ASSESSMENT

As you fill in the blanks below, be honest but nonjudgmental. Track your inner truths and write them for your eyes only. Ultimately, your continuous self-improvement is your own responsibility, so it is essential that you be honest with yourself.

STRENGTHS

Following are my greatest personal assets:

_____

_____

_____

_____

_____

_____

BARRIERS

Now, here are the biggest internal and external barriers I regularly encounter, which keep me from using my personal assets.

_____

_____

_____

_____

_____

_____

SELF-ASSESSMENT (continued)

DESIRED IMPROVEMENTS

List the personal and professional improvements most important to you.

_____

_____

_____

_____

_____

_____

Achieving your "desired improvements" is what this book is about. Be patient with yourself. Work on one or two priority improvements at a time. Once these improvements have been incorporated, move to the next one or two that will expand your self-mastery. Think of ways to overcome the barriers that seem to block you.

Tom's Self-Assessment

"My *strengths* are my enthusiasm, excellent sense of humor, selling ability, interest in other people, love of family and friends, and belief in computers."

"My *barriers* are impatience with things I cannot control, resisting tasks I do not like, avoiding conflict in relationships."

"My *desired improvements* are many! First, I would like to learn a concept such as TQM, to improve things at work. I would also like to handle intimacy better, especially with my wife. I would like to tell my father what I really think and feel."

A NEVER-ENDING PROCESS

Continuous improvement implies a never-ending process. However, changes we make require breaking down our habits into processes we can measure. We eat a meal and when it ends we can count the calories. Think of self-improvement as the orchestration of many smaller processes.

Each of these has a beginning, a middle and an end. Each stage in a process has unique characteristics. Consider the question, "Where should you begin your quest for personal quality improvement?" If you decide you want to spend more time planning and writing, and less time reading and in aimless conversation, recognize that selecting any starting point for change activates resistance to that change. You might begin by observing how much time you currently spend planning and writing. Do you have time to manage your time?

THE BEGINNING

Beginning anything requires redirection of energy and motivation. As we seek the first stage of change, we face two immediate decisions: what to change and how to create energy to overcome barriers to the change. Does it seem like a lot of work? Change is not easy.

THE MIDDLE

The middle stage is characterized by momentum. During the middle of any process, energy flows through the process, creating pathways and patterns to its steps and changes. As our energy flows through a process, large and microscopic transformations occur. We can change our minds or change our goals. Anything is possible.

THE END

Processes have an end point. Characteristics of the end are disengagement, evaluation and sometimes ambivalent feelings. There may be relief or extreme satisfaction with a job well done. There may also be sadness or regret at separating from an enjoyable engagement, or pain from feeling that the job was poorly done or the process full of defects.

A NEVER-ENDING PROCESS (continued)

Self-improvement—changing our process—requires self-mastery, the optimization of our personal assets. We are masterful when we can accomplish our personal dreams and goals. To achieve this mastery, we need to develop some personal characteristics.

First, we need *self-awareness*: readiness to access past or present information about ourselves. When the questions come up of what kind of person we are and what we want for ourselves, we know where to search for the answers.

Second, we need *self-knowledge*: how well we can answer questions about our physical, social, emotional, intellectual, spiritual, career and personal history. This ability to examine our past provides a basis for comparing personal observations with feedback from others.

Last, we need *self-discipline*: making our behavior conform to our personal dreams and goals. This is the energy we expend to control our thoughts, feelings and actions. The past is with us. Artists and psychologists have eloquently described our repetition compulsions to us when we have failed to complete significant, traumatic unions or separations—events from our past. If we can acknowledge and assimilate our past, especially our painful past, we can better assess where we are now, and decide what we want and how to take positive steps on our journey.

Past, present and future are important facets of ourselves that we must respect and try to balance. Take time to think about your past. Now complete the Personal Questions and Answers.

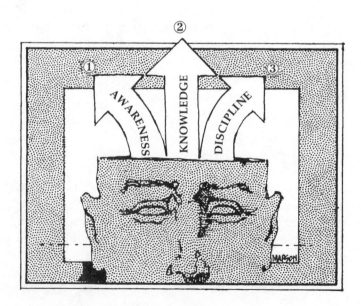

SELF-DISCOVERY EXERCISE

Answer the following questions as honestly as you can. Then see the author's note following this exercise.

1. Where were you born? _____

_____

2. Where were your parents born? _____

_____

3. Where were your grandparents born? _____

_____

4. Name the three most influential teachers in your life—they need not be from formal education

    a. _____

    b. _____

    c. _____

5. Your basic philosophy on life can be summarized as follows: _____

_____

_____

6. You feel most creative when: _____

_____

_____

7. Your closest relationship is with: _____

SELF-DISCOVERY EXERCISE (continued)

8. Things that make this relationship work include: _____

_____

9. List three skills you have mastered:

a. _____

b. _____

c. _____

10. List three skills you would like to master:

a. _____

b. _____

c. _____

11. Who do you feel is most responsible for your present character?

_____

12. What gives you the most joy? _____

_____

13. What is your idea of the greatest fun? _____

_____

14. You feel your greatest asset is: _____

_____

_____

15. You think your worst habit is: _____

_____

_____

16. Following is your belief about your ability to change: _____

_____

_____

17. Things that motivate you the most include: _____

_____

_____

18. Describe a situation that would cause you to celebrate and describe the celebration:

_____

_____

_____

_____

_____

_____

Author's Note:

Take time to read your answers carefully. Think about what you wrote. What did you discover about yourself? Are there items in your life you want to change? Do you believe that change is possible? What about your areas of strength? Can you think of ideas to capitalize more on them? If you have a particularly close friend or mentor, you might wish to share this exercise with that person. The goal is positive self-discovery.

DEFINING PERSONAL QUALITY

The self-assessment you completed is extremely important. Think about a trusted friend who would be willing to help you follow through on your improvement plans. Working with another on personal change greatly increases our chances of turning trials into habits.

You are the greatest asset you can contribute to your organization, your family and your quality relationships. Therefore, it is wise to invest in yourself and to appreciate yourself as an asset. Motivated people produce up to 70 percent more than those who do not care. Self-discipline can give us positive healthy habits, and help us cope with stress and change. As we invest time, thought and energy examining our work and personal productivity, we create enormous potential for finding and eliminating waste, useless frustration and pain. We can use the insight of self-knowledge and the tools of continuous quality improvement to study and improve ourselves.

Most people want "quality." But defining personal quality and its importance in our work and life are tasks as complex as we are.

Some people would describe a quality person as someone worth knowing, a real, caring, competent human being, a person open to continuous growth and development.

After reviewing your self-assessment and self-discovery answers, what personal qualities do you seek:

1. _____

2. _____

3. _____

4. _____

5. _____

Who are the customers of our improved personal qualities? We are. So are our spouses, parents, children, family, friends, neighbors, fellow employees, bosses, customers and strangers.

SALLY'S CHALLENGE

Sally is eager to move from a clerical job to a professional position in a large corporation. She works hard, likes to read, takes courses towards a degree in business, and finds time and energy her biggest barriers. Sally lists ten books she wants to read. How can Sally find time and energy to make career progress?

What are Sally's strengths: _____

_____

_____

_____

What are Sally's barriers: _____

_____

_____

_____

Who are Sally's customers: _____

_____

_____

_____

What would you tell Sally: _____

_____

_____

_____

_____

P A R T

3

Deming, Continuous Quality Improvement and You

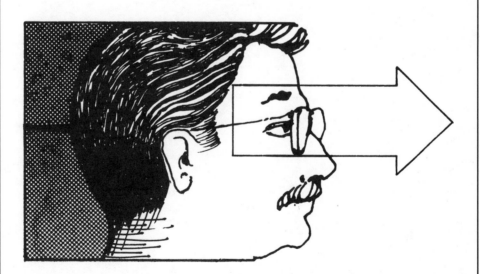

The worldwide quality movement was born in 1950, as Japan lay in ruin, its economic and industrial base destroyed. Dr. W. Edwards Deming, a prominent American statistician, was summoned by General Douglas MacArthur to help with Japan's census. Deming's wisdom was known by several Japanese scientists, who invited him to present his ideas to the Japanese Union of Scientists and Engineers.

DEMING'S QUALITY CHAIN REACTION

Deming's message was so powerful that the leaders invited him back to present his concepts to the chief executive officers of Japan's leading companies. Japan's industrial leaders included Nissan, Toyota and Mitsubishi, among others. They were all struggling to survive, and were deeply impressed with Dr. Deming and his message. With tenacity and patience, the CEOs of Japan's 45 leading companies began the arduous process of learning the principles of continuous quality improvement and putting them into effect.

What was the message that put Japanese industrial leaders at such an advantage?

Deming told them that customers do not want junk. Consumers will pay for quality products. Managers must focus their primary attention on improving the quality of the goods and services they produce. To provide jobs and stay in business for the long term, to improve productivity, eliminate mistakes and delays in the short term, they must improve quality. Deming's "Quality Chain Reaction" predicted the fate of those early followers:

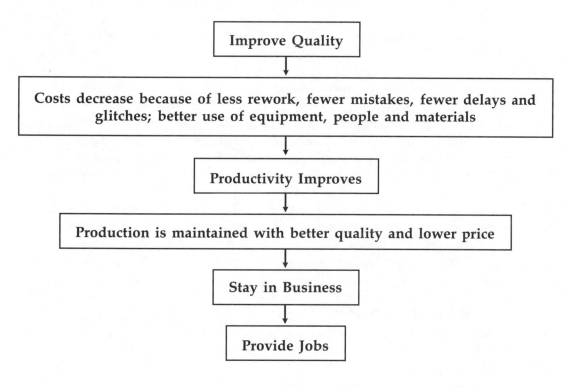

(Deming, 1989)

THREE KEYS TO QUALITY

Deming emphasized three keys to understanding this new philosophy of improving quality.

1. All work is part of a process.

We all have customers and suppliers, internal and external to our business.

2. All processes contain variation.

We must work to understand the variation in the work we do. As we monitor and chart our work processes, we can see and understand the natural variation of the processes we work on. Then we can monitor our improvements.

3. People are the key.

People doing the work are the experts who know where waste is. An environment must exist where everyone feels it is in their own best interest to improve work processes and eliminate waste in the system.

Continuous Quality Improvement (CQI) embodies a new way of perceiving and managing the interactions between suppliers and customers, and all the people, facilities, materials, equipment and processess that work together to produce results. CQI grows out of systems thinking, with an emphasis on continuous feedback from all internal and external customers. Changes in supplies—for example, cheaper fabric to cover chairs—may result in cheaper costs to the customer. However, it may also result in lower durability, higher customer complaints and unanticipated costs, such as equipment adjustment or breakdown to handle lower textile capabilities, and lost repeat sales.

Our world is constantly changing. Products that met needs last year sometimes become obsolete. How can we know how to design, deliver and continuously upgrade products and services? How can we keep up with technological advances, information proliferation and global competition? What questions must we ask and answer?

We must study and learn from our customers, our competitors, our friends, our neighbors, government, researchers—any and all sources—now and forever. Is that why the major Japanese exporting corporations have been so successful?

Industry has been very good at developing new technology in the form of equipment and tools. Complex computerized engineering and geological logging techniques, robotics in automobile manufacturing and satellite telecommunications speed messages across the globe in seconds.

However, industry has not been nearly as good at developing new methods in the way people like us attack and solve routine problems we encounter every day. Deming blames top management for ignoring their full responsibility for the quality of products and services their organizations produce. He teaches that top managers must understand four kinds of profound knowledge to achieve customer-driven quality:

1. Knowledge of the organization as a system

2. Knowledge of variation and prediction

3. Knowledge of the root causes of variation

4. Knowledge and ability to motivate people

Although these concepts were written for businesses, the basic ideas apply to individuals as well. How can an organization sustain change, transform the way it designs and produces products and services, if its people do not internalize profound knowledge?

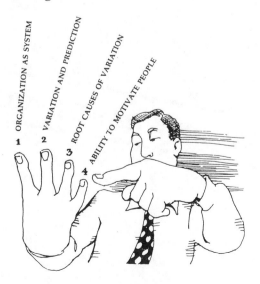

DEMING'S METHODOLOGY

Dr. Deming worked with Dr. Walter A. Shewhart at Bell Laboratory in New York in the 1920's. He learned from Shewhart the power of statistical method to provide information about the accuracy and precision of industrial processes. Quality of the process could not be improved until sufficiently accurate and precise data indicated that the process was under statistical control. Shewhart created the use of control charts to track agricultural and industrial processes for quality control.

Deming and Shewhart scrupulously taught their students the following principles:

1. The statistician's levels of significance furnish no measure of practical prediction.

2. Industrial data presentation must include not only numerical data but also who observed, type of measurement equipment and materials used, method of recording the observations, temperature and humidity, description of efforts made to reduce error, etc.

3. The only reason to carry out a test of process data for accuracy and precision is to improve a process, and to improve the quality or quantity of the next production run or crop. (Shewhart, 1986)

The Shewhart Cycle is a simple way of breaking down the continuous quality improvement process into a series of small experiments:

The Shewhart Cycle

Step	What It Involves	For Example
1. PLAN	a. Design the change as an experiment. b. Review data, ask the experts, conduct background study.	a. Delores and the other associates will analyze where their customers live and work and target direct mail advertising to bring them in for their next sale. b. Ask store staff for their other ideas; review sales records; ask customers for input.
2. DO	a. Try to change under controlled conditions. b. Be sure to isolate the particular process you are attempting to improve.	a. Tom gathers the mailing lists and sends direct mail invitations to the sale. b. He avoids telephone calls this time and maintains his print advertisement in the city newspaper.
3. CHECK	a. Measure the results of the change. b. Identify other important questions to answer or improvements to try.	a. Tom and staff identify by zip code targeted customers who buy at the sale. b. They want to know how to track others who came in but did not buy.
4. ACT	a. Based on the above results, improve the process or system. b. Repeat the cycle as many times as you want and need to.	a. Tom makes repeat business a top priority and feels a little more confident. He buys everyone lunch and publicly thanks Delores. She seems pleased.

UNDERSTANDING THE PROCESS

Why have statisticians had such a dramatic impact on improving quality? The answer to that question is directly related to a shift in thinking that Deming teaches us is necessary to make.

We must first understand the process we want to improve. That means we must use measures to track results—production, on-time delivery, unit sales, etc. Once we run the process and measure its results, *if* we analyze the most likely reason for variation in those results, we have begun a shift in thinking.

The statistician wants to answer these questions about our results:

1. What measures did you use?

2. Are your instruments the right ones?

3. Do the instruments work properly?

4. What were the detailed procedures used, and who gathered the data?

5. Given the number of total results and the range of variation, is the process stable?

If your process is not stable, there is no predictable way to improve it.

If your process is stable, variation within it is random. The cause of variation in a stable system is called a COMMON CAUSE. A stable system produces outcomes with a predictable amount of variation. We describe its production as its system capacity.

Shewhart's control chart is a statistical method for distinguishing between controlled and uncontrolled variations due to common cause, and special causes.

Controlled variation—common cause—reflects random process results based upon all of the variables in the system. Controlled variation is "the system." Think about variation in the gross national product of the country. What accounts for upward or downward changes? Economists and philosophers may espouse theories of cause, but in most countries such variation is random and part of the system's capability.

Shewhart also observed variation of a different type, which he called "special cause." Special cause variations are results that occur outside the expected upper or lower limits of a stable system. If the stock market dropped 1,000 points, most people would see that as a special cause. If you played golf on the weekend and made a hole-in-one, how would you account for that result?

Remember the importance of common and special cause analysis of process results. The most successful Japanese manufacturers do.

Deming taught that the only way to improve process results in a stable system is to redesign the system. That is the core of CQI and requires systems thinking. So does self-improvement. Quick fixes do not last, at work or at home.

Special causes are much easier to isolate and remove. If production declined due to a power outage from a heavy storm, would that be in the system or a special cause?

Are flat sales in Tom's store a common or special cause process result?

Common causes of variation are usually the responsibility of management to correct and often need more detailed analysis to isolate.

A DEFINITION OF QUALITY

The key word in continuous quality improvement is *quality*. Continuous quality improvement emphasizes the design and delivery of quality products and services to all customers, internal and external. Quality is usually defined as *meeting or exceeding customer expectations, with value added.* Quality requires conformance to customer requirements, ultimately, through products and services without waste or defects. With quality comes customer satisfaction; less rework, lost sales and waste; lower production costs and increased market share.

The Joiner Triangle

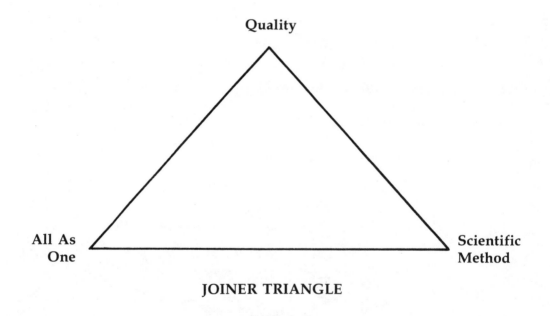

JOINER TRIANGLE

The Joiner Triangle (Scholtes, 1989) shows three important parts of the continuous quality improvement process. It illustrates that quality depends on sound, scientific principles and everyone working together. Of course, the definition of quality changes. Products and services without defects may delight us now, but often become obsolete tomorrow. So quality is a constantly changing goal.

The scientific method is an important tool to help us achieve quality. Continuous quality improvement implies a series of scientific experiments, designed to study important aspects of the processes of our work that influence what we produce for customers. What is new about this? Before we leap to conclusions about the obviousness of this principle, consider the strength of traditions, superstition, appearance, illusion, beliefs and stereotypes on our organizations and on us. CQI demands we study ourselves and research theory and root causes to examine possible explanations, subsequently we must carefully design experiments to observe, gather data and test our hypotheses so that we may make improvements based upon prediction.

For example, when we count calories, weigh ourselves regularly, study the caloric content of our usual meals, modify our diet based on calories, fat and fiber content, then the anticipated weight gains, losses or stability are predictable. How much will we weigh after the holiday season? Why? Who controls this process? If we know the scientific principles, what accounts for our behavior?

Social learning research indicates that people's expectations strongly influence their reported perceptions. Even when we generate possible reasons for why events happen, we have great difficulty seeing information that differs from what we have seen before. We have the ability to objectively study our habits. However, the decision to study and change our behavior requires self-discipline, patience, and an expanded self-perception. Change is often difficult.

The third point of the Joiner Triangle is ''all as one.'' Continuous quality improvement requires teamwork and cooperation. This, too, is difficult in our culture. Most large corporations have a forced ranking system to compensate and reward employees rated superior to their peers. When we live or work in a culture of individual contribution, seeking quality, using the scientific method and working ''all as one'' are very difficult behaviors for most of us.

Human factors play a major role in all work, especially in the successful operation of complex equipment, such as supersonic jet aircraft. When we climb into the cockpit, we must already have the learned competence to read and interpret the many dials and to control the aircraft.

Application of scientific methods to manufacturing, process management and all aspects of human performance provide the core CQI message. We must also understand the CQI messenger.

WORKING WITH PEOPLE

Psychology helps us to understand people and our interactions with others and circumstances within any system of management. The four main points to working with people include:

1. People learn in different ways and speeds.

2. Leaders have an obligation to make changes in the system of management that will bring improvement.

3. Intrinsic motivation is critical to all people.

4. Everyone is unique.

Even though everyone is unique, all people need some of the same things, such as relationships with other people, love and esteem from others and self-esteem and respect. Circumstances provide some people with dignity and self-esteem and deny other people these advantages. Management that denies its employees dignity and self-esteem will smother their intrinsic motivation.

Management must be sure it rewards employees appropriately. If it depends on a reward system outside the employees' control, the system may:

- not reward but rob employees of dignity and self-esteem

- tempt and reward employees for doing what they know is wrong for higher pay or ratings

- neutralize intrinsic motivation

This results in high stress for employees and low productivity or quality for the company. It need not be so. Employees naturally want to learn and be innovative and enjoy their work.

THE CONTINUOUS QUALITY IMPROVEMENT PHILOSOPHY

Continuous quality improvement requires an operating philosophy to support it. In addition to the points of the Joiner triangle, other factors are crucial to such a philosophy:

► Removing the causes of problems in the system leads to improved quality and productivity.

► People doing the job are most knowledgeable about that job.

► People want to be involved, do their jobs well and feel like valued contributors.

► Adversarial relationships between labor and management are counterproductive.

► Structured problem-solving processes, using graphical techniques, produce better solutions than unstructured processes.

► Every organization has breakthroughs waiting to be discovered.

"The quality movement is the first industrial change that is based on the importance of people thinking, where brains are more critical than machines."

Lloyd Dobyns & Clare Crawford-Mason
Quality or Else (1991)

SYSTEM OPTIMIZATION

A system is a series of activities within an organization that work together for the aim of the organization. Components are usually interdependent, necessary for system improvement and share a stake in the organization's gain.

When a system is optimized, everyone works together to accomplish the organization's aim. When that happens, everybody gains. When we ignore others in our organization and concentrate only on our part, overall quality suffers. This can be called "suboptimization." Organizations must be managed and their boundaries adjusted to optimize any system. Suboptimization causes loss to everybody in the system.

> "The components of a system could in principle under stable conditions, manage themselves to accomplish their aim."
>
> W. Edwards Deming

An optimized system recognizes differences between employees, customers and managers in a workplace where employees take joy in their work, free from fear of ranking.

TOM'S SALES

Why have sales in Tom's store remained even for the past seven months? Tom wondered about the economy, his PC products, his staff and his own performance.

He brought his staff together to see what ideas they had. Tom still felt defensive about his own performance.

Delores suggested that they try writing to their most loyal customers. She said she has been helping several of her long-time customers to upgrade their systems. Tom wasn't so sure this was the best plan, but he decided to go along with the test.

TRANSFORMING MANAGEMENT

Deming listed 14 points for transforming the management of organizations. Transformation of management could then lead to a transformation of work.

---

1. Create constancy of purpose—a statement to all employees of the organization's aims and purposes, which is reflected in management's actions.

2. Learn the new philosophy.

3. Understand the purpose of inspection: to improve processes and reduce cost.

4. End the practice of awarding business on price alone.

5. Improve constantly and forever the system of production and service.

6. Institute training for skills.

7. Teach and institute leadership.

8. Drive out fear, create trust and a climate for innovation.

9. Optimize toward the aims and purpose of the organization, the efforts of teams, groups and work units.

10. Eliminate exhortations or slogans for the work force.

11. Learn the capabilities of processes and how to improve them.

12. Remove barriers that rob people of pride in their skills.

13. Encourage education and self-improvement for everyone.

14. Take action to accomplish the transformation.

PART

4

Personal Applications of the Deming Principles

Personal applications of the Deming principles give us tools to help us develop professionalism about *ourselves*. This increased self-awareness can be a tremendous asset at work, as we learn to better understand our power and influence, to identify what we want and negotiate ways to please ourselves and our customers. Everyone is our customer, including ourselves.

WHAT IS PROFOUND SELF-KNOWLEDGE?

Profound self-knowledge recognizes that:

1. Each person is a system.

2. Everyone is different and everyone is affected by variation; prediction can help us increase self-mastery.

3. We must question and find the root causes why we think, feel and do what we do.

4. We do what we want or need most to do, which ranges from survival to self-actualization and spirituality, depending on our life situation.

Everyone's situation is different. Variation is constant. We need to understand the reason for variation, the type of variation in our work processes and systems. We can also study the reasons for variation in our personal processes. We can study our personal habits, preferences, where and when we spend our time, money and emotional energy. We can try to understand some personal processes we own.

One excellent way to learn about ourselves is to use standardized measures. Individual assessment instruments are many and varied. It is often extremely helpful to objectively assess one's social styles, values, vocational interests, technical knowledge, interpersonal skills, vocabulary and many other attributes against one's peers and one's self-perceptions. Use whatever instruments you wish to calibrate your current state of knowledge and self-mastery.

PERSONAL APPLICATIONS OF DEMING'S PRINCIPLES

Deming's principles of transforming management can be applied to your personal situation. Ask yourself the following questions:

1. What is your purpose, mission or vision of what you want? How well does it align with your organization's purpose? What are you willing to do to align and adapt to your work mission? What are you willing to do to accomplish your personal goals? You will have a chance to work on your constancy of purpose in Part 5.

2. How well do you understand the philosophy of continuous quality improvement? What is your philosophy of life? For personal quality standards to have any meaning, you must learn and apply them.

3. What is your impact on your customers? Understand the value of self-observation to identify personal processes to study and improve. If you do your part perfectly, can your product or service still have defects? You can use our senses to inspect work and personal processes. Inspection alone does not yield quality.

4. What are the true costs associated with buying the "cheapest" of everything? What is the cost of quality? Are you getting the best value for your money and time? Usually you get what you pay for. End the practice of buying products and services on the basis of price alone.

5. What can you do to improve yourself as a system? Think at a system-design and improvement level and commit to improving *constantly and forever* what you and your system produce for your customers. Understand that you are a system, too: a collection of vital organs, a brain, memories and experiences, learning and an individual point of view. Do you take care of your body, mind and spirit? Quick fixes usually fail to alter long-term problems. Keep an open mind.

6. Do you have the skills you want and need? Do you have the optimal environment for learning new skills? Are you able and willing to develop your skills? Mastery takes time, energy, and some previous knowledge and ability. There is no substitute for motivation.

7. Are you willing to follow another's leadership? Are you comfortable with your self-leadership skills? Do you want to lead others? What do you want to learn about leadership? You are the chief executive officer of your individual thoughts, habits and relationships. You usually do what you really want to do.

8. What do you fear? How do your past and present fears affect your vision of yourself and the future? Whom do you trust? Who trusts you? How do you nurture trusting relationships? Explore the ''volcano within'' in Part 5.

9. How willing are you to understand and cooperate with other people? How well do you optimize your time and energy at home and at work? What are you doing to optimize your organizational roles? Our colleagues and bosses are customers with whom we can choose to cooperate and satisfy.

10. Do you tell people what you think they should do, *before* attempting to understand their position? How do you react to slogans, especially when they are directed at process outcomes outside of your control? Give yourself positive messages. You are a unique, wonderful and capable person. It is okay not to be perfect.

11. What processes do you own? How well do you understand the way you think, act and work? What data-gathering tools do you use to study and improve your personal and work processes? Use the CQI tools that follow to investigate potential improvements.

12. What gives you pride? What gives you ''pride of skill''? How can you create energy to do the things most important to you? Nothing can surpass a customer you have delighted or a masterpiece you have created!

13. What do you want to learn? What aspects of yourself do you want to improve? Where are you in your self-improvement, personal-development process? We will develop a plan in Part 7.

14. How empowered do you feel to accomplish personal and work improvements? What actions are you taking? What actions remain to be taken? Keep reading and working. You can do it!

CQI TOOLS YOU CAN USE

An extremely valuable part of the quality revolution is the use of problem-solving techniques that rely heavily on the additive brain power of teamwork and graphical tools. CQI tools can make your situation clear, show you your options and indicate the relative importance of various circumstances, and whether your choices have had any effect.

Continuous quality improvement tools include flow charts, check sheets, pareto charts, cause-and-effect diagrams, run charts, histograms and control charts.

FLOW CHART

A flow chart is a picture that represents steps in a process. Flow charts help us think about how work moves through these steps, where delays occur, the decisions involved and the relationship between steps. We will limit our flow chart to these simple symbols:

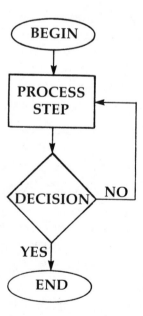

Flow charts often help us better understand a complicated process, such as buying a house or planning a large party. Flow charting often identifies steps and details we might neglect. It may also help us simplify the process. Continuous quality improvement tools graphically identify opportunities for improvement; we still must supply the motivation to complete the process.

TOM'S FLOW CHART OF PC MAINTENANCE

How can Tom simplify this process?

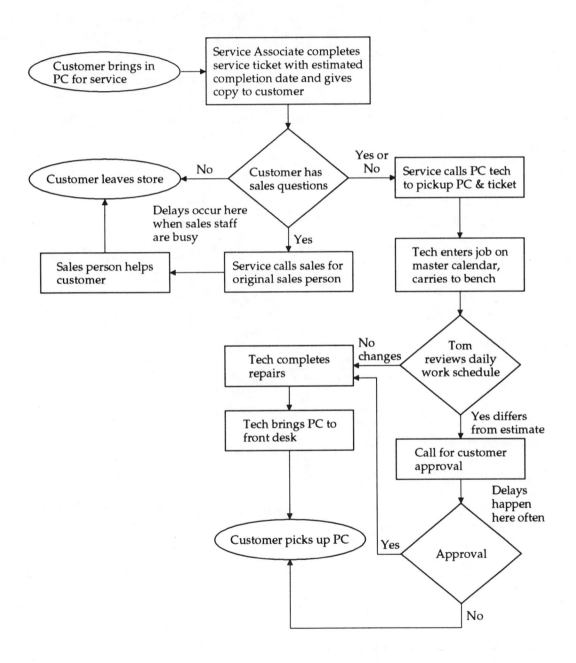

Flow Chart Example

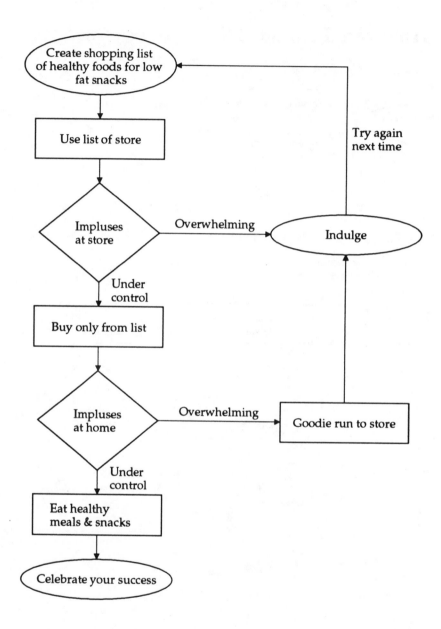

Refer to the list you developed and try flow-charting a personal process that you indicated you wished to improve. Use the space below to create your flow chart.

CHECK SHEET

A check sheet is a simple form used to discover how often something happens. It helps us apply scientific observation to situations that might otherwise be dominated by strong, unsupported opinions.

Quantification requires that the data be gathered in a uniform manner and the data sample be representative of the entire class and time span—every day of every month.

For example, you may feel that you need another telephone line or a cellular phone. Before you invest in the additional expense, you could track your telephone calls.

CALLS	JANUARY					
	5	6	7	8	9	TOTAL
INCOMING	////	//	⊮ ⊮	⊮ ⊮ ⊮	//	33
OUTGOING	///	///	⊮ /	⊮ ⊮	///	25
TOTAL	7	5	16	25	5	58

Should you buy another telephone? You now have information that can help you decide. Refer to your list again and create your own check sheet for a personal process improvement in the space provided below:

Observation	Check Each Occurrence							Total
	1	2	3	4	5	6	7	
Example: Use stairs at work	|	|||		||	||||			10

PARETO CHART

A Pareto chart is a vertical bar graph that displays the frequency of a problem from the highest bar, to the next highest, and so on. Pareto charts are very helpful for choosing which problems to address in what order. Once we choose a starting point for problem solving, usually we must delve deeper for the likely causes of the observed problems.

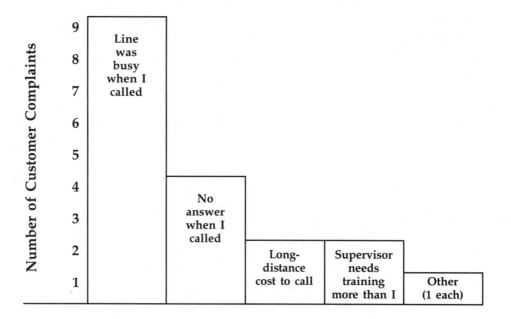

This Pareto chart shows customer complaints about telephone service. Notice how most of the customers complained about the same thing—the line was busy when they called.

The Pareto Principle is often presented as the 80–20 rule. Eighty percent of our problems come from 20 percent of our customer situations, such as the above telephone capacity and coverage problem. Think of your diet. Do 80 percent of your unwanted calories come from 20 percent of your food items?

The Pareto principle identifies the "significant few," such as our chocolate snacks and the late-night ice cream binges, rather than the "trivial many," the fruits, vegetables and nutritious foods we eat.

Personal improvement can be a tough game. We can add more telephone lines if we can afford the cost. However, it is a lot harder to eliminate sweets in our diet.

TOM'S PARETO CHART

Pareto analysis is one of the easiest and most powerful ways of using CQI to improve a process. Often we must study our work to determine where we are spending our time and money. If Tom's store expenses are increasing slightly and his income from sales remains constant, how can he find the best way to maintain profitability?

Tom can ask the experts, his store staff. He can also analyze where they are spending their expense money to find the largest opportunity for savings. Here is a typical Pareto analysis of his monthly expenses:

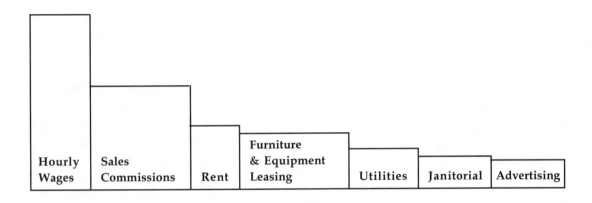

Where would you advise Tom to search for more detailed information to help him control expenses?

_____

_____

_____

_____

_____

_____

_____

_____

_____

HISTOGRAM

A histogram is a bar graph of a frequency distribution in which the bars are different measurements and the height of the bars show the number of occurences of that measurement. Here is a histogram of grades from a class of 16 students.

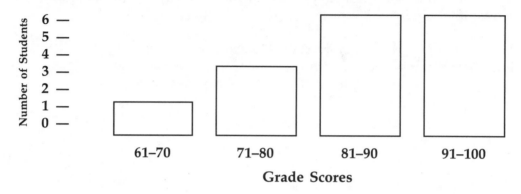

TOM'S HISTOGRAM

Tom and Delores decided to study the frequency distribution of repeat customers and their average monthly sales volume. Here is a histogram of their findings.

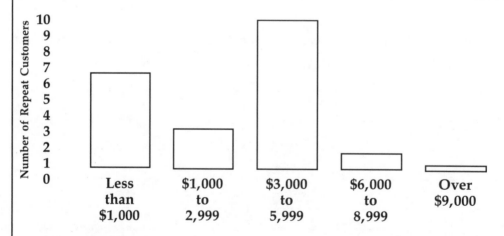

Average monthly sales from repeat customers at Lightspeed Computer Store over the past seven months.

How might Tom and Delores further analyze the market potential of their repeat customers?

Can you think of a way that a histogram would help you in the improvement of a personal process?

RUN CHARTS

A run chart is a measurement over time or sequence. Run charts give us a clear picture of the variation within a system. They monitor a process and chart how the long-range average changes. Data is graphed in the order it becomes available. We expect variation above and below the average, and the run chart helps us identify trends.

Typical industrial examples might include how many days it takes a company to deliver a product, from the day it was ordered, temperature or pressure of a vessel or defects per manufacturing run. Measured variation on run charts provides the scientific data that enables us to predict the expected variation in a stable process. This prediction is called *statistical process control*.

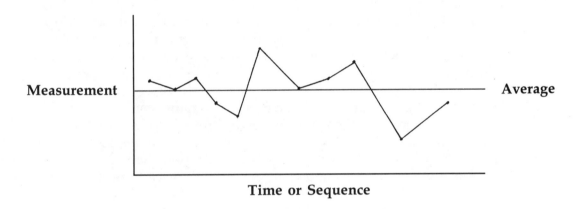

Run charts have many useful personal applications: calorie count, expenditures, exercise miles or minutes, telephone calls, correspondence, pages written of your novel—the list is endless.

Here is a run chart of daily calories consumed by an average adult male:

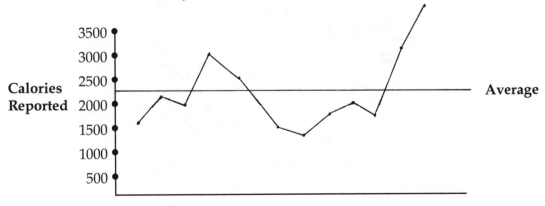

PERSONAL QUALITY IMPROVEMENT

Each person must decide what quality means for them individually and for their customers. We will concentrate on exercises to build the specifications or ''whats'' of our own personal quality improvement. Remember—even when our customers or spouse tell us what they expect from us, we must decide to listen and to try to find a way to deliver what they want. Quality involves personal choices from top to bottom. Will you read the dial correctly or fudge the results? That's a typical quality decision. Do you want to please your customers or spouse, parents or children? Or do you really prefer to compete with them, to gain their attention, recognition, love, anger or rejection, to fulfill your inner expectations?

Every daily decision you make is an opportunity to transform yourself. Most of us know that transformation comes from the inside out. For example, we must decide to count calories, manage our eating and exercise to maintain our health and fitness.

Respected authority figures might encourage us or communicate messages that we interpret as rejection. What we choose to ''hear'' is always selective, limited by our sensory equipment, previous learning expectations and our physical and emotional state. Our challenge is to accept our built-in subjectivity, and to push forward and choose a starting place for self-mastery.

You have chosen to read this book. You also have considerable control over other choices. We all can redirect our thoughts and actions. Taking control and responsibility for your personal quality improvement can only be done by you as an individual no matter how hard others push or pull you.

PERSONAL PROCESSES TO IMPROVE

List below personal processes you would like to improve. For example, you might choose to exercise weekly, to reduce fat grams and calories in your weekly diet, to say positive messages to yourself and others, to keep on a monthly budget, to play the saxophone regularly. After you decide what and how to pursue personal quality improvement, work with a peer you trust to help you practice your improvements. With mutual feedback, the changes you both seek are much more likely to last and become positive habits.

I intend to improve the following personal processes:

_____

_____

_____

_____

_____

_____

_____

_____

_____

_____

_____

_____

_____

_____

_____

Next we will dig deeper to identify personal interference in the full use of our potential. Exercises will help us focus on past, present and future dynamic issues in our personal ''volcano.'' We will focus on continuous learning and improvement at work and home.

P A R T

5

Your Personal
Path for
Self-Mastery

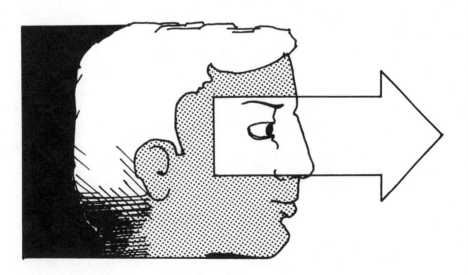

We can choose to use tools of the scientific method to help us define quality, gather data, ask and answer questions, make business and personal decisions, and measure our progress. Also embedded in our brain are personal memories, experiences, beliefs, values, vulnerabilities, emotions and attitudes that easily and often distort our ability to separate ourselves from our best business and personal choices.

CARRYING OUR PAST INTO THE FUTURE

Our personal path for self-mastery will weave us back and forth between past, present and future. We want to minimize the waste we bring into our business and personal life. Many of us carry experiences like excess baggage: unresolved relationships, feelings and beliefs. When we interpret an event as a personal loss, our emotions master *us* and we struggle to control our panic, fear, pain, rage and shame. Human beings are imperfect sensing instruments, yet the best of us are capable of saintly self-discipline, scientific and artistic genius, and unconditional love. With practice and patience, you can control how you respond to the world.

The following exercises were designed to help you identify how you see yourself, important relationships and their past, present, and future potential significance to you. Spend time thinking about your life's journey up until the present. Your childhood, family, friends, triumphs and tragedies, fears and dreams, habits and health form part of your uniqueness. These exercises were designed to help you identify personal applications, small experiments you can choose to track your path for a continuously improving you.

The totality of you is the gift you may bring your work associates, your relatives, your closest friends and yourself.

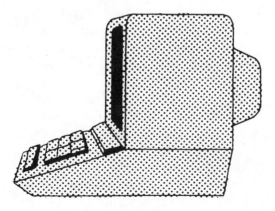

EXPLORING THE VOLCANO WITHIN

We are all on a journey. Some believe this journey is eternal. Others feel their journey lasts as long as they live. Some do not give much thought to their journey.

The journey is life, and we travel it as an individual self. What does having a self mean? How do we develop and improve as a self? Is it ever *too late* for us to change and improve ourselves?

Psychologists agree that self-improvement is always possible. This is because each individual is responsible for his or her choices. As an individual, you make your important life decisions. You are a self-renewable asset. With self-mastery, you alone determine the scope and breadth of your potential contributions.

When you were conceived, your parents' chromosomes created a genetic roadmap, filled with challenges and abundant human potential. When you were born, the dramatic interplay between your genetic potential and the world's uncertainties began.

We know the profound impact of infancy on human development. What we become can be nurtured—or retarded or even destroyed.

Illness, accident, disease and environmental forces—often beyond our control—can threaten our safety and the development of our maximum potential. Elements such as these can inhibit our sense of self.

Family life has changed over the years—yet, we all need quality, nurturing relationships. What are your memories and feelings about your childhood? Did you feel loved? Or do childhood memories fill you with pain? Were you abused? Did you feel neglected, underappreciated? Underloved? The journey to a continuously improving self leads each person into "the volcano within," and into the future, too.

We all begin life vulnerable and dependent on others. We are also born with individuality, will, energy and, to one degree or another, a hunger to overcome our barriers. We are predisposed to master the human development tasks of walking, talking, learning, working with others and loving. We learn formally, as students in school, and through our experience and our life choices. We know that who we are now is closely related to who we were yesterday and all the yesterdays we knew before today.

Many psychologists believe that human beings can turn their genetic potential into action; adults can transform themselves; they can choose to develop self-mastery through self-discipline, self-understanding and self-knowledge.

ZONE 1: PSYCHO-SOCIAL TAPES

We are on that journey together. Our personal yesterdays form our own buried energy, our personal volcano.

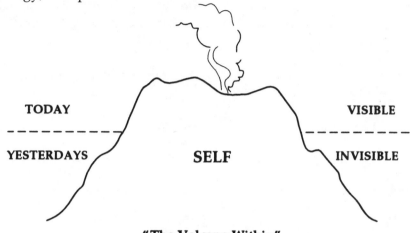

TODAY

YESTERDAYS   **SELF**   **VISIBLE**

INVISIBLE

"The Volcano Within"

We can harvest our energy by examining what's inside ourselves. As we self-explore, we will always connect with today. We will seek questions to answer about yesterdays, where we are now and where we want to go to create the future we want.

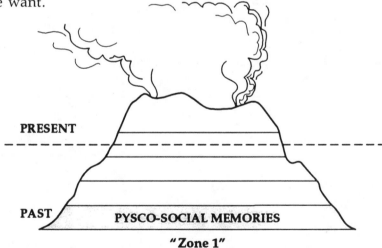

PRESENT

PAST   **PYSCO-SOCIAL MEMORIES**

"Zone 1"

Our first excursion is deepest into the volcano, Zone 1. Here is where our total sensory experience is stored. These are our psychosocial tapes, our memory of how we grew and how others responded to our uniqueness. This is where information resides about how we use our will, impulse and feelings to learn and adapt to the world. Deep in Zone 1 is information on what you were like as a child and on who from your past has been most important to you.

The following page contains an exercise to help you recall important perceptions and relationships that shape and guide your personal and work life.

EXERCISE: SELF-DESCRIPTION

Below are important stages in your development characterized by the words *child, teenager, new employee, now,* and *future.* Take a few minutes for each item and complete a brief self-description. Do not worry about what you say or how you write your thoughts and feelings. Try to capture your core impressions of yourself.

Complete the following sentences and add whatever other thoughts you want to help others better understand you.

My impressions of what I was like as a child are: _____

_____

_____

_____

My impressions of what I was like as a teenager are: _____

_____

_____

_____

My impressions of what I was like as a new employee are: _____

_____

_____

_____

My impressions of what I am like now: _____

_____

_____

_____

My impressions of what I will be in the future: _____

_____

_____

_____

SOME OF TOM'S IMPRESSIONS

. . . as a child: "I was hyper, eager to please, into electronic and mechanical things."

. . . as a new employee: "I wanted to succeed, probably seemed cocky, knew I could sell."

. . . what I will be in the future: "More relaxed and patient, eager to learn, a better husband and father, an industry sales leader."

Write below what you learned from your self-description:

_____

_____

_____

The next exercise helps us identify and examine our most important relationships. Think about the other person. Take time to consider your view of the relationship, what you want from the other person, what you want to give, and your present interpersonal skill to get or give what you want.

TOM'S RELATIONSHIPS

"I often took my mother for granted, while I sought my father's approval. She has always been there for me and my girls."

EXERCISE AHEAD

EXERCISE: IDENTIFY THE RELATIONSHIPS MOST IMPORTANT TO YOU

- List the people.
- Describe the relationship.
- Write what you want most from each person.
- Write what you want to give each person.
- Rate your skill in getting and giving the above in these relationships.
- List any questions you want to ask others about the past.

Tom's Response

Person	Relationship	What I Want	Want to Give	Skill to Get/Give
Mother	Adult, some loneliness, love, mutual respect	Unconditional love, understanding of my life circumstances	Love, support for passage to older years and health problems, adult caring	Getting better past few years, usually avoid "hooks"

Your Response

Questions to ask:

EXERCISE: IMPORTANT RELATIONSHIPS— PAST, PRESENT, AND FUTURE

1. Complete the following:

Important Relationships	Past Significance	Present Significance	Questions to Answer
Example: Grandparents	Lived in my home for 10 yrs; gave me feelings of tradition and family continuity.	Since their death, I have missed the closeness and strength of my family.	How can we celebrate the traditions and joys of our family?

2. If possible, with a selected partner, discuss the influence of past relationships and events on your work and life.

3. Think about your whole life, your family, health, childhood, education, friendships, sports, hobbies, triumphs, failures, and list "personal glossary" words that characterize the inner you.

Example: self, Stamford, baseball

My words _____

_____

_____

_____

EXERCISE: PERSONAL GLOSSARY

To better understand me, I would like you to know the following important words from my personal vocabulary and the meaning **I** give to each:

WORD	MY PERSONAL MEANING
Example 1: Self	The individual I am, carrying my history, culture, values, feelings, ideas and full potential for growth and improvement in all I do, and in the quality of my feelings.
Example 2: Stamford, CT, USA	Where I spent 12 important years growing up and learning family personalities and values—my adopted ''home town.''
Example 3: Baseball	My favorite sport; a perfect game; symbol of life's dramatic, joyous journey; never over until the last out!
Add Your Own:	

EXERCISE: IDENTIFY THE RELATIONSHIPS MOST IMPORTANT TO THE ORGANIZATION

Rate the importance of the following to your organization (5 is most important and 1 is least important):

Spouse		1 2 3 4 5
Children		1 2 3 4 5
Parents		1 2 3 4 5
Friends		1 2 3 4 5
Boss		1 2 3 4 5
Teachers		1 2 3 4 5
Spiritual leader		1 2 3 4 5
Peers		1 2 3 4 5
Subordinates		1 2 3 4 5
Customers		1 2 3 4 5
Suppliers		1 2 3 4 5
Strangers		1 2 3 4 5
Me		1 2 3 4 5

Write below your reasons for the above ratings:

_____

_____

_____

_____

_____

_____

Tom rated *Boss, Customers, Suppliers, Subordinates, Strangers,* and *Me* most important to Lightspeed Computers. He wondered about the conflict in values with his most important relationships, *Spouse, Children,* and *Parents.* Should such conflicts be resolved?

ZONE 2: EMOTIONS, PAST AND PRESENT

Our next excursion is into the zone of our emotions, past and present.

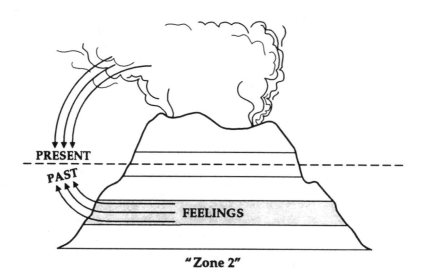

"Zone 2"

Each person has a hierarchy of needs. We process sensations through the filter of both our emotions and our intellect. Our will, impulses and feelings have the potential to be thwarted by others who are bigger, more experienced or more powerful.

We grow by learning to postpone immediate need gratification, and gradually develop trust that in time our needs will be satisfied. As we grow, we store emotional energy. Feelings energize us, and at other times torture us. As children, we feel intensely. We sometimes struggle to understand our boundaries. If our parents divorce, abuse or neglect us, we blame ourselves for the hurt, pain or shame we feel.

Our feelings have enormous power—power to help us align with others, build quality relationships, improve our lives—and power to fester, distort our perceptions, consume and waste our energy and destroy our capacity for wisdom and maturity. Unexpressed feelings at work can destroy our motivation and productivity.

Excursion two will help us begin the process of separating our feelings from the feelings of others.

EXERCISES: SITUATIONS AND COPING WITH OUR EMOTIONS

PURPOSE

The purpose of these exercises is to help us to think about the power of emotions to motivate and distort our thoughts about and interactions with others.

DESIRED OUTCOMES

As a result of these exercises, we should have:

1. A list of persons, situations, places or institutions that "hook us." They often serve as flash points or blind us from objectivity.

2. A list of people and situations that usually bring out the best in us.

3. Increased understanding of the desirability of separating our feelings from those of others, in our personal and business relationships.

4. Increased understanding of the power of direct communication, including recognition of underlying feelings, to keep relationships in a win-win zone.

5. A list of strategies for coping positively with our vulnerabilities.

EXERCISE: BEST AND WORST FEELINGS

1. List below people or situations that bring out your emotional worst:

Person, Situation	Usually Brings Out These Thoughts, Feelings or Actions
Example: Paying bills	"We're doomed, on our way to the poorhouse," moodiness, inadequacy, yell at the dog

2. List below those people or situations that often bring out your best:

Person, Situation	Usually Brings Out These Thoughts, Feelings or Actions
Example: Jogging or walking	"I'm O.K.," competent, confident, pet the dog

EXERCISE: ALTERNATIVE FEELINGS

Think about these positive and negative situations. Select one or more alternative strategies for coping with your vulnerabilities. Do we have the power to change our thoughts? Yes! Try hard and good luck.

Alternative Strategies

Thoughts	Feelings	Actions
Example: "I owe so much money."	I am okay because I pay my bills; I am adding to the economy.	Think long-term. List my assets. Ask my spouse to pay the bills.

EXERCISE: RELATIONSHIPS AND EMOTIONS

Review the material you developed for the previous Exercises. Now think about and complete the following statements:

	Past	Present	Future
Important Relationship	*This person made me feel . . .*	*Now when I am with this person I feel . . .*	*When I think about or interact with this person, I would like to feel . . .*
Parent			
Spouse or Significant Other			
Boss			
Customers			

EXERCISE: COMFORT AND VULNERABILITIES MATRIX

List below the topics, situations or interpersonal relationship issues you are comfortable communicating to important others. Specify who those ''important others'' are in your life.

Next list your vulnerability zones for the same issues and with the same people:

Topic, Situation, Relationship Issue	Important Other(s)	Comfort Zone	Vulnerability Zone
Example 1: Body weight	spouse, parents, children, friends	silence	feel fat, defensive
Example 2: Relating to supervisor(s)	supervisor, second line manager	talking, negotiating the concepts, work tasks, products	being left out, lack of incentives and rewards, feeling devalued

Add Your Own:

TOM'S EXERCISE RESULTS

TOM'S FEELINGS

Tom had trouble completing these exercises. He believes that he bought into the myth of man as hero. Tom wrote, ''My father and most authority figures bring out my worst. I expect rejection, so I try to act smart or funny.''

Tom asked Mary, his wife, to help him understand how he ''reacts.'' They spent hours of quality time together. Tom began to realize that his emotional withdrawal was sending messages of disappointment and inner pain to Mary and his daughters. He also realized that just as Tom with his father, they probably interpreted his ''stuff'' as rejection.

Mary enjoyed listening to Tom. Tom in return appreciated Mary's insights. They were both learning that feelings *are* facts.

ZONE 3: VALUES AND BELIEFS

Our next excursion is to Zone 3, our values and beliefs. The people who are important to us have strongly influenced our core values and beliefs, our paradigms of right and wrong, true and false, good and bad.

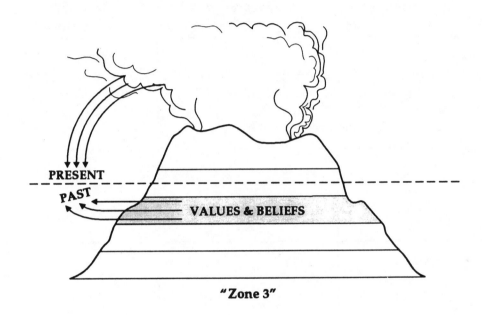

PRESENT

PAST

VALUES & BELIEFS

"Zone 3"

The rapidly changing world challenges our beliefs. From our experiences, we have formed beliefs about ourself. Does yesterday's self-concept fit today's you?

Think of a volcano. Its past is on the surface. Its present is molten, potential energy, beneath the surface. Our values and beliefs, too, are a source of enormous energy for continuous improvement. If we think about our core principles and act on them, we often practice different habits.

Certainly, we learn our earliest beliefs from our parents, then from family, religious leaders, teachers, community culture and important others. What is the impact of this early learning on us now?

Throughout history, individuals have chosen to fight, die and kill others for their beliefs. What values and beliefs are sacred to you? How willing are you to re-examine your beliefs? How willing are you to change them?

EXERCISE: VALUES AND BELIEFS

Think about your most strongly held values and beliefs, those ideas that guide your life. List them below from past, present and future.

My Most Strongly Held Values and Beliefs:	Learned From: (Past and Present)	What It Would Take to Change: (Present and Future)
Example: People are born good and deserve the chance to grow and develop to their maximum potential	Parents, human development research, religious teaching, social work principles	Nothing, I hope. Perhaps a catastrophe with a young sociopath
1.		
2.		
3.		
4.		

How can we find ways to coexist and negotiate win-win agreements with people whose core values and beliefs differ from our own?

Examine the core values and beliefs of your friends and colleagues. Try this exercise with them. What might you learn about your own beliefs?

ZONE 4: THOUGHT AND INTELLECT

Our next excursion is closer to the surface of the volcano, Zone 4, the zone of thought and intellect. Percolating with potential energy are thoughts, dreams, fantasies, visions, discoveries, ideas, concepts, innovations, questions, answers, learning, skills and habits.

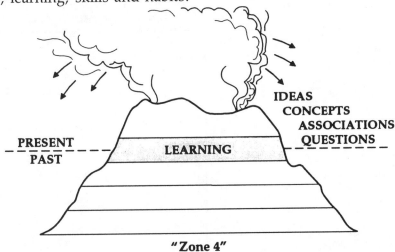

PRESENT
PAST

LEARNING

IDEAS
CONCEPTS
ASSOCIATIONS
QUESTIONS

"Zone 4"

To use Zone 4 effectively, we must constantly stir our ideas, test our hunches, adopt new learnings, try new habits, adopt new ways to think, work and question why. If we do not do this, we may choke our potential to understand. We must learn and relearn, continuously stimulate our ideas, and consciously plan to think about ourselves and our work processes at a level high enough to accept new paradigms about ourselves and our work and adapt to new information about each.

This is often difficult. Expressing innovative ideas may place us in the role of change agent. New ideas challenge the system and threaten people, especially people in power positions. New ideas may threaten us, as well as our perception of ourselves and the way things "should be."

Ideas can also be intoxicating. Sometimes, just because we can, we will tamper with a person or process and cause an unanticipated eruption of problems and pain. Evidence from industrial psychology, the employee empowerment movement and case studies from business, entertainment and the arts show us that we possess the power to transform ourselves. Often the appearance of innovation is really the changing of the palace guard.

The mastery of learning is essential to the mastery of quality relationships. Both are necessary to support our motivated actions for continuous improvement. Our ideas create energy for our vision of our desired future state. We must continuously align our personal and business mission and core values with our visions.

EXERCISE: LEARNING

Let's examine what and how we stimulate our knowledge of ourselves and the world.

Past	What I Remember Most Vividly
1. My best year(s) in school:	
2. My best teacher(s):	
3. Most influential book(s):	
4. Most influential movie(s) or play(s):	
5. Most significant learning:	

Present	What I Want to Improve
1. I learn best from:	
2. Books I am reading now:	
3. Courses/seminars/workshops I have taken or will take in the next 12 months:	
4. My most important mentor is:	

EXERCISE: LEARNING (continued)

Future	How I Will Make It Happen
1. My ideal learning situation:	
2. Books I want to read:	
3. Learning experiences I want:	
4. Habits I want:	
5. What I want to teach others:	

ZONE 5: THE CONTINUOUSLY IMPROVING SELF

The surface of the volcano that is the continuously improving self is Zone 5. We choose to run or walk or sleep. We bloom where we're planted, or we curse our lot in life.

As with molten lava, our actions and interactions with the physical world, our environment, and within our relationships with other people can reshape or burn, create mountains or tidal waves. Our actions can harden and become enormous barriers to ourselves and other people. This zone is also where our unresolved feelings, prejudices and historical hang-ups explode and rain fire and ash on ourselves and the rest of the world.

What is our vision of the future?

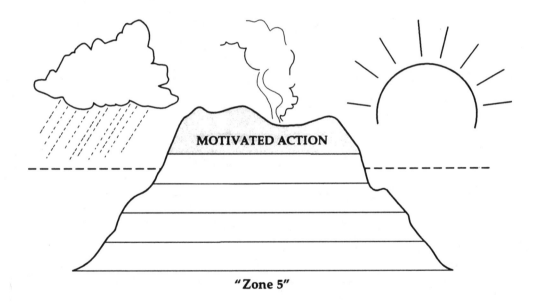

"Zone 5"

Continuous self-improvement means energy applied to measurable, self-chosen areas of a person's thoughts, learning, feelings and behavior that is observed and recorded, regardless of apparent results.

We have the power to improve ourselves. It is our choice.

ZONE 5: THE CONTINUOUSLY IMPROVING SELF (continued)

Different people envision the future in different ways. Some may see it as a place; others may see it as a condition. Our vision can serve as a rope from the future that can help guide us through the troubled waters of the present to our dreams.

Personal missions often flow directly from our vision, values and beliefs. What do you dream of doing? What do you dream of becoming?

You may want to clarify your personal mission. What do you see as your purpose in life?

_____

_____

_____

_____

_____

_____

_____

_____

_____

_____

_____

_____

_____

These exercises bridge the past, present and future by drawing from us our future vision, personal mission, wants and goals. Remember, we usually get what we expect.

Take as much time as you want to complete the exercises on the facing page.

EXERCISE: VISION, MISSION, WANTS AND GOALS

This is my vision of where I would like to be in three to five years:
(*Example:* well-respected, international consultant and teacher)

_____

_____

_____

My personal mission is:
(*Example:* help others achieve quality results through learning)

_____

_____

_____

This is what I want for myself:

(*Example:* quality time with my family; worldwide travel; satisfied customers; excellent health; loving friends; continuous learning)

_____

_____

_____

To accomplish my mission, vision and wants, my long-term goals are:

Example: 1. Study, research and learn by taking at least three formal courses and workshops a year.
2. Publish at least one book and three articles a year.
3. Celebrate all major family events with parents, wife, children and grandchildren.

_____

_____

_____

_____

MOTIVATED ACTION FOR CONTINUOUS IMPROVEMENT

Considering your personal vision and mission, think about and answer the following questions. This additional self-assessment may help frame where you can concentrate some energy to overcome obstacles in your path towards a continuously improving self. Think long-term; think about your future.

LONG-TERM GOALS

List below your most important long-term goals and the internal and external barriers you must overcome to achieve them:

| | Barriers | |
Goals	Internal	External
1.		
2.		
3.		
4.		

Consider the external barriers you listed above. Identify some strategies for overcoming them. For example, if your creative ideas are blocked by an unresponsive supervisor, consider cosponsoring the idea with your supervisor; or go to another supervisor, get neutral feedback about your idea; or seek help from a friend.

SELF-OBSERVATION PLAN

In the space below, write the relationship, person, situation and personal actions you will take for each. There are many excellent daily, weekly and annual planners (see Crisp Publications *Successful Self-Management* and *Personal Time Management*) you can use. We usually get what we measure. Now review your notes from the exercises and plan regular actions:

TOM'S PLANS

Person/Situation	Personal Action	When
Father	Tell him I want his opinion and approval	During Sunday calls
Alicia Lightspeed	Support TQM efforts by sharing marketing questions	Next regional meeting

YOUR PLANS

Person/Situation	Personal Action	When
1.		
2.		
3.		
4.		
5.		

P   A   R   T

6

Quality Relationships

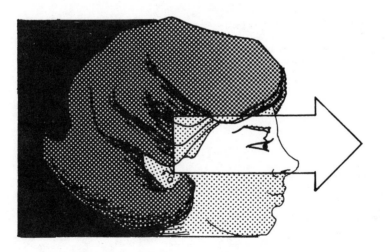

Our relationships have unique importance. They are the principal, if not exclusive, source of real happiness. There is no substitute for investing time and energy with people, building relationships and investing in our mutual emotional bank accounts.

CONTINUOUS IMPROVEMENT THROUGH QUALITY RELATIONSHIPS

Relationships have predictable processes. They have beginnings, middles and endings. Relationships have dynamic challenges, because they so often involve union or closeness with others, and separation or differentiation from others. We meet our most intimate needs through relationships. This invests them with great emotional currency and substantial risks.

Quality relationships are characterized by mutual respect and controlled emotional involvement. They are not characterized by absence of emotion. Self control and patience with others are important ingredients in relationship-building. Creating energy in our relationships requires self-discipline, and avoiding dumping or projecting our feelings and needs on the other person. We must concentrate energy on being more sensitive to the emotional needs of others, to understand and respond appropriately to those needs in our interactions with others.

SEVEN PRINCIPLES FOR A QUALITY RELATIONSHIP

To create emotional acceptance, we should help others by working on the following seven principles, necessary for a quality relationship:

1. Accept each person as a unique individual.

2. Give the person a chance to express his or her positive and negative feelings.

3. Respect the dignity and self-worth of each person by controlling your emotional involvement—remain objective, concentrate on the other person and do not get defensive.

4. Accept others where they are, listen to each person and respond with understanding.

5. Maintain a nonjudgmental attitude toward others who may misunderstand or disagree with our ideas.

6. Respect the right of others to make their own choices (even when you think you have a better idea).

7. Build trust. Respect the confidentiality of personal feelings or of other personal information shared with you.

Note: Consider both your personal and professional roles. Discuss them with your spouse or a close friend. Do you see each other the same way?

QUALITY RELATIONSHIP PROFILE

How well do I do this in my personal and professional roles?

	Do all the time	Do often	Do some time	Do rarely	Do never
1. Accept the individual.	1	2	3	4	5
2. Enable purposeful expression of feelings.	1	2	3	4	5
3. Maintain self-controlled emotional involvement.	1	2	3	4	5
4. Accept others where they are.	1	2	3	4	5
5. Maintain a nonjudgmental attitude.	1	2	3	4	5
6. Respect the right of others to make decisions.	1	2	3	4	5
7. Build trust by keeping personal information confidential.	1	2	3	4	5

Be Honest in Your Answers.

TOM'S QUALITY RELATIONSHIP PROFILE

	Do all the time	Do often	Do some time	Do rarely	Do never
1. Accept the individual.	1	②	3	4	5
2. Enable purposeful expression of feelings.	1	2	3	④	5
3. Maintain self-controlled emotional involvement.	1	②	3	4	5
4. Accept others where they are.	1	2	③	4	5
5. Maintain a nonjudgmental attitude.	1	2	3	④	5
6. Respect the right of others to make decisions.	1	2	3	④	5
7. Build trust by keeping personal information confidential.	1	②	3	4	5

''I keep personal information private. I have trouble dealing with people I perceive as making stupid decisions. Unfortunately, this includes myself, my wife, my parents, my staff and customers. I plan to ask others at work and at home to ask me to express my feelings if they want to know them. I will also keep a daily checklist of these principles and review my progress weekly.''

QUALITY RELATIONSHIP PRACTICE AND FEEDBACK

1. Ask your spouse or close friend to suggest ways you may demonstrate one or more of the seven principles with them.

2. Track each important relationship in a journal. Write principles you are doing all of the time, often, sometime, rarely and never. Plan time for each principle, especially those you have trouble with.

3. Write a note to the important person, expressing appreciation for helping you or spending valuable time with you.

4. Repeat or do the ''Important Relationship'' exercises from Chapter 5.

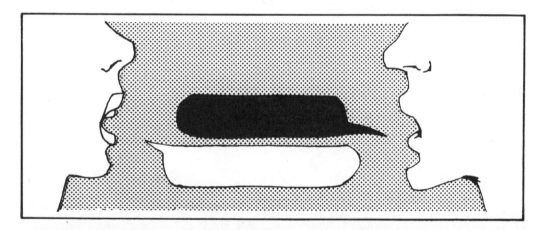

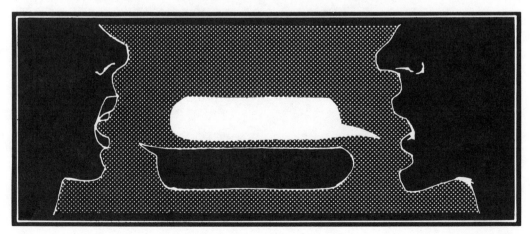

P A R T

7

Continuous Learning

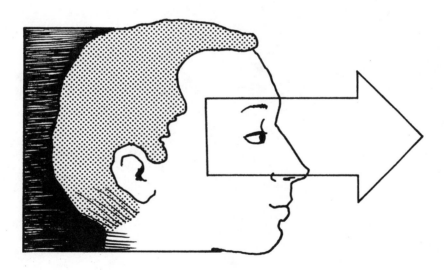

We are an infinitely curious species. Once our security and survival needs are met, most people seek social affiliation, influence over and recognition from others, and a sense of competence and achievement. As our world shrinks, our need to process, store and use complex knowledge increases.

CONTINUOUS LEARNING FOR A CONTINUOUSLY IMPROVING YOU

We seek knowledge, skills and entertainment. We also seek ways to understand and interact with ourselves, friends, strangers, people we love, people we fear, and spiritual and philosophical aspects of our thoughts. Dr. Deming emphasized that managers must constantly seek to ''know the unknowable.'' He deeply respects the power of profound knowledge and the intrinsic curiosity and ability of people to learn.

Everything we want for ourselves activates barriers. If we want to run a marathon, we must overcome many barriers. These barriers are internal and external. There are also many resources to help us learn ways around them: books and other media, friends who have relevant knowledge and experience, experts and observation. What is your marathon?

CONTINUOUS LEARNING FOR A CONTINUOUSLY IMPROVING YOU (continued)

Our adventure with life unfolds every day. Each day gives us new energy, opportunities for creativity, work, loving and learning. Every obstacle we encounter gives us the spark to envision ways around it. Resistance we meet to the goals we set is a gift. Barriers help us concentrate our plans and energy to get what we want. Seek to learn what you want and what barriers these wants will encounter.

What makes barriers a "gift"? _____

_____

_____

_____

_____

Everyone is different. We all learn differently. Describe the best way to continue your own learning:

_____

_____

_____

_____

_____

_____

_____

Something I Want to Learn

Media/Method:	Best for Me:	Who, What, When:
1. Books		
2. Journals/Magazines		
3. Television		
4. Videos		
5. Games		
6. Software		
7. Conversations with a Mentor Tom's Example:	✔ good	"Talk to Mother about her parenting hints"
8. Travel/Visits		
9. Meditation		
10. Seminars or Formal Classes		
11. Other:		

CONTINUOUS LEARNING (continued)

We have discussed four types of profound knowledge. What questions, additional courses or training do you want, so you can address each part of profound knowledge?

Profound Knowledge	My Questions, Desired Courses or Training
1. Appreciation of System	(*Example:* How do managers best fit individuals in organizations to please their customers?)
2. Theory of Variation	(*Example:* What are the major threats to validity in my sampling techniques?)
3. Theory of Knowledge	(*Examples:* Beginning Conversation Spanish, History of Music courses)
4. Psychology	(*Example:* How much more productive are ''empowered'' employees? How does one persist in a life-long exercise program? How does one say no to a French pastry?)

THE RACE WITH NO FINISH LINE

Congratulations! You have come far on your journey to a continuously improving self. Keep on with the journey. You will benefit most from this book if you periodically review your answers, excursion responses and personal quality improvement exercises. Share what you want with another improving self. Continue to learn yourself, master yourself, love and improve yourself, and you may create your future.

BIBLIOGRAPHY

Anonymous. "Productivity awards show importance of employee involvement." *Worklife Report* (Canada), V6, N5, 1989.

Argyris, C. "Teaching smart people how to learn." *Harvard Business Review*, May–June, 1991.

Ball, Carolyn M. *Claiming Your Self-Esteem.* Berkeley, CA: Celestial Arts, 1990.

Biestek, Felix. *The Casework Relationship.* Chicago: Loyola University Press, 1957.

Bennett, J. G. *The Sevenfold Work.* Charles Town, West Virginia: Claymont Communications, 1979.

Bennett, J. G. *Transformation.* Charles Town, West Virginia: Claymont Communications, 1978.

Bennett, J. G. *The Dramatic Universe.* Volume 1. Revised Edition. Charles Town, West Virginia: Claymont Communications, 1987.

Bennett, J. G. *The Dramatic Universe.* Volume 3. 2nd Claymont Communications Edition. Charles Town, West Virginia: Claymont Communications, 1987.

Berne, Eric, M.D. *Games People Play.* New York: Grove Press, 1964.

Bone, Diane & Griggs, Rick. *Quality at Work: A Personal Guide to Professional Standards.* Los Altos, CA: Crisp Publications, Inc., 1989.

Bowman, Joseph C. "Leading by example." *Quality Progress,* V22, N11, 38–41, November, 1989.

Bowman, Joseph C. and Brady, Linn M. "Dow Chemical, Texas, project makes continuous improvement part of everyone's job." *Industrial Engineering,* V20, N8, 40–45, August, 1988.

Buscaglia, L. *Living, Loving & Learning.* New York: Fawcett Columbine, 1982.

Byham, William C. & Cox, Jeff. *Zapp: The Lightning of Empowerment.* Pittsburgh: Development Dimensions International Press, 1989.

Conway, William. "William Conway On The Right Way To Manage." *Quality Progress.* January, 1988.

BIBLIOGRAPHY (continued)

Covey, Stephen R. *The 7 Habits of Highly Effective People.* New York; Simon & Schuster, 1989.

Covey, Stephen R. *Principle-Centered Leadership.* Provo, Utah: Institute for Principle-Centered Leadership, 1990.

Crosby, Philip B. *The Eternally Successful Organization: The Art of Corporate Wellness.* New York: Plume, 1990.

Deming, W. Edwards. *Out of the Crisis.* Cambridge, MA: Massachusetts Institute of Technology, Center for Advanced Engineering Study, Ninth Printing, 1989.

Dobyns, Lloyd; Crawford-Mason, Clare. *Quality or Else: The Revolution in World Business.* Boston: Houghton Mifflin Co., 1991.

Faatz, A. J. *The Nature of Choice in Casework Process.* Chapel Hill: University of North Carolina Press, 1953.

Fisher, R. and Ury, W. *Getting To Yes: Negotiating Agreement Without Giving In.* New York: Penguin Group, 1983.

Fossum, Lynn. *Understanding Organizational Change.* Los Altos, CA: Crisp Publications, 1989.

Gadon, Herman. "Making sense of quality of work life programs." *Business Horizens,* V27, N1, 42–46, January–February, 1984.

Gagne, R. M. *Studies of Learning: 50 Years of Research.* Tallahassee: Learning Systems Institute, 1989.

Glasser, W. *Control Theory: A New Explanation of How We Control Our Lives.* New York: Harper & Row, 1984.

Greenwald, H. *Direct Decision Therapy.* San Diego: Edits Publishers, 1973.

Guaspari, J. *I Know It When I See It: A Modern Fable About Quality.* New York: AMACOM, 1985.

Hall, Douglas T. & Isabella, Lynn A. "Downward movement and career development." *Organizational Dynamics,* V14, N1, 5–23, Summer, 1985.

Hersey, Paul; Blanchard, Kenneth H. *Management of Organizational Behavior: Utilizing Human Resources.* 5th Ed. Englewood Cliffs, N.J.: Prentice Hall, 1988.

Jaffe, Dennis T. & Scott, Cynthia. *Empowerment.* Los Altos, CA: Crisp Publications, 1989.

Jaffe, Dennis & Scott, Cynthia. *Managing Organizational Change.* Los Altos, CA: Crisp Publications, 1989.

Kanter, R. M. "Change: where to begin." *Harvard Business Review,* July–August, 1991.

Keen, Sam. *Fire in the Belly: On Being a Man.* New York: Bantam Books, 1991.

Kieth-Lucas, Alan. "A critique of the principle of client self-determination." *Social Work,* July, 1963.

Lee, Chris. "Beyond teamwork." *Training,* 25–32, June, 1990.

Lickson, J. "Using sensitivity in representing a public assistance agency to help an AFDC mother make fuller use of service." Unpublished MSW practice project, University of Pennsylvania School of Social Work, 1966.

Lynd, H. M. *On Shame And The Search For Identity.* New York: Science Editions, Inc., 1961.

Maddux, Robert B. *Team Building: An Exercise in Leadership.* Los Altos, CA: Crisp Publications, 1992. Revised Edition.

Martin, William B. *Managing Quality Customer Service.* Los Altos, CA: Crisp Publications, 1989.

May, R. *The Courage To Create.* New York: Bantam Books, 1990.

Merrill, A. Roger and Merrill, Rebecca R. *Connections: Quadrant II Time Management.* 2nd Printing, 1990. Salt Lake City, Utah: Publishers Press.

Moustakas, C. E. and Jayaswal, S. R. Editors. *The Self: Explorations in Personal Growth.* New York: Harper & Row, 1956.

Peck, M. D., M. Scott. *The Road Less Traveled.* New York: Simon and Schuster, 1978.

Post, Frank G. M. "Beware of your stakeholders." *Journal of Management Development,* V8, N1, 28–35, 1989.

Price, F. "Out of bedlam: management by quality leadership." *Management Decision* (U.K.), V27, N3, 1989.

Rank, Dr. Otto. *Will Therapy & Truth and Reality.* New York: Alfred A. Knopf, 1964.

Scholtes, Peter R. *The Team Handbook: How To Use Teams To Improve Quality.* Madison, WI: Joiner Associates, Inc. Fourth Printing, 1989.

Senge, Peter M. ''The leader's new work: building learning organizations'' *Sloan Management Review,* Fall, 1990.

Shewhart, Walter A. *Statistical Method from the Viewpoint of Quality Control.* New York: Dover Publications, Inc., 1986 (Reprint of 1939 publication).

Timm, Paul R. *Successful Self-Management.* Los Altos, CA: Crisp Publications, 1987.

Viorst, J. *Necessary Losses.* New York: Fawcett Gold Medal, 1986.

Walton, Mary. *The Deming Management Method.* New York: Pedigree Book, 1986.

Zemke, R. ''Personal growth training: maybe it can't hurt, but can it help?'' *Training Magazine,* V15, N7, July, 1978.

Zuboff, Shoshana. *In the Age of the Smart Machine: The Future of Work and Power.* New York: Basic Books, Inc., 1988.

The author welcomes reader feedback to continuously improve these ideas, examples, and exercises.

I especially liked: _____

_____

_____

_____

My suggestions for improvement: _____

_____

_____

_____

As a result of this book, I: _____

_____

_____

_____

I would like more information about The Training Consortium workshops for organization, management, and personal skills improvement: ☐

You Name (optional): _____

Organization: _____

Address: _____

City, State, Zip: _____

Telephone/Fax number: _____

Please mail or fax to:

    Jeffrey E. Lickson, Ph.D.
    The Training Consortium
    10555 Northwest Freeway, Suite 215
    Houston, Texas 77092

    Fax number: (713) 681-5034

NOTES

FOR OTHER FIFTY-MINUTE SELF-STUDY BOOKS
SEE THE BACK OF THIS BOOK.

NOTES

FOR OTHER FIFTY-MINUTE SELF-STUDY BOOKS
SEE THE BACK OF THIS BOOK.

NOTES

FOR OTHER FIFTY-MINUTE SELF-STUDY BOOKS
SEE THE BACK OF THIS BOOK.

NOTES

FOR OTHER FIFTY-MINUTE SELF-STUDY BOOKS
SEE THE BACK OF THIS BOOK.

$\boxed{\text{FOR OTHER FIFTY-MINUTE SELF-STUDY BOOKS} \atop \text{SEE THE BACK OF THIS BOOK.}}$

NOTES

ABOUT THE FIFTY-MINUTE SERIES

We hope you enjoyed this book and found it valuable. If so, we have good news for you. This title is part of the best selling *FIFTY-MINUTE Series* of books. All *Series* books are similar in size and format, and identical in price. Several are supported with training videos. These are identified by the symbol **V** next to the title.

Since the first *FIFTY-MINUTE* book appeared in 1986, millions of copies have been sold worldwide. Each book was developed with the reader in mind. The result is a concise, high quality module written in a positive, readable self-study format.

FIFTY-MINUTE Books and Videos are available from your distributor. A free current catalog is available on request from Crisp Publications, Inc., 95 First Street, Los Altos, CA 94022.

Following is a complete list of *FIFTY-MINUTE Series* Books and Videos organized by general subject area.

Management Training (continued):

Personal Improvement:

Human Resources & Wellness:

Human Resources & Wellness (continued):

Communications & Creativity:

Customer Service/Sales Training:

Small Business & Financial Planning:

Adult Literacy & Learning:

Career/Retirement & Life Planning: